The Woman's Labour

an epistle to

MR STEPHEN DUCK

in answer to his late poem called

THE THRESHER'S LABOUR

by

MARY COLLIER

and published here with

THE THRESHER'S LABOUR

by

MR STEPHEN DUCK

RENARD PRESS

RENARD PRESS LTD

Kemp House
152–160 City Road
London EC1V 2NX
United Kingdom
info@renardpress.com
020 8050 2928

www.renardpress.com

The Woman's Labour: An Epistle to Mr Stephen Duck first published in 1739
The Thresher's Labour first published in 1730 (revised in 1736)
An Elegy Upon Stephen Duck and *An Epistolary Answer to an Exciseman* first published in *Poems on Several Occasions* in 1762
This edition first published by Renard Press Ltd in 2021

Edited text, Note on the Text, Notes and Selection © Renard Press Ltd, 2021

Cover design by Will Dady

ISBN: 978-1-80447-005-3

All rights reserved. This publication may not be reproduced, stored in a retrieval system or transmitted, in any form or by any means – electronic, mechanical, photocopying, recording or otherwise – without the prior permission of the publisher.

CONTENTS

The Woman's Labour   5
  by Mary Collier
    Advertisement   7
    The Woman's Labour   9
    The Three Wise Sentences Taken from
      The First Book of Esdras   21

The Thresher's Labour   39
  by Stephen Duck

An Elegy Upon Stephen Duck   55
  by Mary Collier

An Epistolary Answer to an Exciseman
Who Doubted Her Being the Author   57
  by Mary Collier

  Notes   61
  Note on the Text   61

THE WOMAN'S LABOUR

an epistle to

MR STEPHEN DUCK

in answer to his late poem called

THE THRESHER'S LABOUR

to which are added

THE THREE WISE SENTENCES

taken from

THE FIRST BOOK OF ESDRAS

ch. III *and* IV

by

MARY COLLIER

now a washerwoman at

PETERSFIELD IN HAMPSHIRE

ADVERTISEMENT

IT IS THOUGHT PROPER to assure the reader that the following verses are the real productions of the person to whom the title page ascribes them.

Tho' she pretends not to the genius of Mr Duck, nor hopes to be taken notice of by the great, yet her friends are of opinion that the novelty of a washerwoman's turning poetess will procure her some readers.

If all that follow the same employment would amuse themselves and one another during the tedious hours of their labour in this, or some other way as innocent, instead of tossing scandal to and fro, many reputations would remain unwounded, and the peace of families be less disturb'd.

I think it no reproach to the author, whose life is toilsome, and her wages inconsiderable, to confess honestly that the view of her putting a small sum of money in her pocket, as well as the reader's entertainment, had its share of influence upon this publication. And she humbly hopes she shall not be absolutely disappointed; since, tho' she is ready to own that her performance could by no means stand a critical examination, yet she flatters herself that, with all its faults and imperfections, the candid reader will judge it to be something considerably beyond the common capacity of those of her own rank and occupation.

MARY COLLIER
1739

Immortal Bard! thou fav'rite of the Nine!*
Enrich'd by peers, advanc'd by Caroline!*
Deign to look down on one that's poor and low,
Remembering you yourself was lately so;
Accept these lines: Alas! what can you have
From her, who ever was, and's still a slave?
No learning ever was bestow'd on me;
My life was always spent in drudgery:
And not alone; alas! with grief I find,
It is the portion of poor womankind. 10
Oft have I thought, as on my bed I lay,
Eas'd from the tiresome labours of the day,
Our first extraction from a mass refin'd,
Could never be for slavery design'd;
Till time and custom by degrees destroy'd
That happy state our sex at first enjoy'd.

THE WOMAN'S LABOUR

When men had us'd their utmost care and toil,
Their recompense was but a female smile;
When they by arts or arms were render'd great,
They laid their trophies at a woman's feet;   20
They, in those days, unto our sex did bring
Their hearts, their all, a free-will offering;
And as from us their being they derive,
They back again should all due homage give.

Jove,* once descending from the clouds, did drop
In show'rs of gold on lovely Danaë's* lap;
The sweet-tongu'd poets, in those generous days,
Unto our shrine still offer'd up their lays:
But now, alas! that golden age is past;
We are the objects of your scorn at last.   30
And you, great Duck, upon whose happy brow
The muses seem to fix the garland now,
In your late poem boldly did declare
Alcides'* labours can't with yours compare;
And of your annual task* have much to say –
Of threshing, reaping, mowing corn and hay;
Boasting your daily toil, and nightly dream,

THE WOMAN'S LABOUR

Would vanish soon, and quickly disappear,
Were you, like us, encumber'd thus with care.
What you would have of us we do not know:
We oft take up the corn that you do mow;
We cut the peas, and always ready are
In ev'ry work to take our proper share;   130
And from the time that harvest doth begin,
Until the corn be cut and carry'd in,
Our toil and labour's daily so extreme
That we have hardly ever *time to dream*.

The harvest ended, respite none we find;
The hardest of our toil is still behind:
Hard labour we most cheerfully pursue,
And out, abroad, a-charing often go:
Of which I now will briefly tell in part
What fully to declare is past my art;   140
So many hardships daily we go through,
I boldly say, the like *you* never knew.

When bright Orion* glitters in the skies
In winter nights, then early we must rise;

THE WOMAN'S LABOUR

The weather ne'er so bad, wind, rain or snow,
Our work appointed, we must rise and go;
While you on easy beds may lie and sleep,
Till light does thro' your chamber windows peep.
When to the house we come where we should go,
How to get in, alas! we do not know: 150
The maid, quite tir'd with work the day before,
O'ercome with sleep; we standing at the door
Oppress'd with cold, and often call in vain,
Ere to our work we can admittance gain:
But when from wind and weather we get in,
Briskly with courage we our work begin;
Heaps of fine linen we before us view,
Whereon to lay our strength, and patience, too;
Cambrics* and muslins, which our ladies wear,
Laces and edgings, costly, fine and rare, 160
Which must be wash'd with utmost skill and care;
With Holland shirts, ruffles and fringes too,
Fashions which our forefathers never knew.
For several hours here we work and slave,
Before we can one glimpse of daylight have;
We labour hard before the morning's past,
Because we fear the time runs on too fast.

THE WOMAN'S LABOUR

At length bright Sol* illuminates the skies,
And summons drowsy mortals to arise;
Then comes our mistress to us without fail, 170
And in her hand, *perhaps*, a mug of ale
To cheer our hearts, and also to inform
Herself what work is done that very morn;
Lays her commands upon us, that we mind
Her linen well, nor *leave the dirt behind*:
Not this alone, but also to take care,
We don't her cambrics nor her ruffles tear;
And *these* most strictly does of us require,
To save her soap, and sparing be of fire;
Tells us her charge is great, nay, furthermore, 180
Her clothes are fewer than the time before.
Now we drive on, resolv'd our strength to try,
And what we can, we do most willingly;
Until with heat and work, 'tis often known,
Not only sweat, but blood runs trickling down
Our wrists and fingers; still our work demands
The constant action of our lab'ring hands.

Now night comes on, from whence you have relief,
But that, alas! does but increase our grief;

With heavy hearts we often view the sun,   190
Fearing he'll set before our work is done;
For either in the morning, or at night,
We piece the summer's day with candlelight.
Tho' we all day with care our work attend,
Such is our fate, we know not when 'twill end:
When ev'ning's come, you homeward take your way;
We, till our work is done, are forc'd to stay;
And after all our toil and labour past,
Sixpence or eightpence pays us off at last;
For all our pains, no prospect can we see   200
Attend us, but old age and poverty.

The washing is not all we have to do:
We oft change work for work as well as you.
Our mistress of her pewter doth complain,
And 'tis our part to make it clean again.
This work, tho' very hard, and tiresome, too,
Is not the worst we hapless females do:
When night comes on, and we quite weary are,
We scarce can count what falls unto our share –
Pots, kettles, saucepans, skillets we may see,   210

THE WOMAN'S LABOUR

Skimmers and ladles, and such trumpery,
Brought in to make complete our slavery.
Tho' early in the morning 'tis begun,
'Tis often very late before we've done;
Alas! our labours never know an end;
On brass and iron we our strength must spend;
Our tender hands and fingers scratch and tear:
All this, and more, with patience we must bear.
Colour'd with dirt and filth we now appear;
Your threshing *sooty peas* will not come near.   220
All the perfections woman once could boast
Are quite obscur'd, and altogether lost.

Once more our mistress sends to let us know
She wants our help, because the beer runs low:
Then in much haste for brewing we prepare,
The vessels clean, and scald with greatest care;
Often at midnight, from our bed we rise –
At other times, ev'n *that* will not suffice;
Our work at ev'ning oft we do begin,
And 'ere we've done, the night comes on again.   230
Water we pump, the copper we must fill,

Or tend the fire; for if we e'er stand still,
Like you, when threshing, we a watch must keep,
Our wort boils over if we dare to sleep.

But to rehearse all labour is in vain,
Of which we very justly might complain:
For us, you see, but little rest is found;
Our toil increases as the year runs round.
While you to Sisyphus* yourselves compare,
With Danaus' daughters* we may claim a share; 240
For while *he* labours hard against the hill,
Bottomless tubs of water *they* must fill.

So the industrious bees do hourly strive
To bring their loads of honey to the hive;
Their sordid owners always reap the gains,
And poorly recompense their toil and pains.

THE THREE WISE SENTENCES

From the First Book of Esdras*
Chap. III and IV

In gentle numbers fain my muse would sing
Of great Darius, Persia's royal king;*
That potent monarch, whose imperial sway
So many mighty kingdoms did obey;
From India's coast to Ethiopia's land,
All people did submit to his command.

The King with feasting in most noble sort
Did entertain the princes of his Court,
Till night came on, and all retired were,
Then to his chamber did to rest repair;   10
Where several noble youths strict watch did keep,
To guard his sacred person in his sleep:
Among them three young men of virtuous mind,
Whose hearts to study wisdom were inclin'd,
Had privately, between themselves, agreed

THE WOMAN'S LABOUR

To leave in writing, for the King to read,
What, in their judgements, did in strength excel
All other things, for they discerned well
Their sovereign's bounteous disposition so,
What they could wish, he would on them bestow.   20

The first of them in writing did declare
That *nothing could for strength with wine compare*;
The second then his sentence in did bring:
Nothing for might is equal with the King;
With like assurance did the third decree
*Women do bear away the victory
From all on earth*; but yet he knew full well
Great was the truth that did in heaven dwell.

These papers seal'd, where secretly convey'd
Beneath the pillow where Darius laid,   30
Until Aurora* did her light display,
And Phoebus,* rising, usher'd in the day;
Then they withdrew, and when the King did rise,
His servants on the writings cast their eyes,
And to his sacred majesty made known

THE THREE WISE SENTENCES

What in the night had by his guards been done.
The King was pleas'd on hearing the report
How the brave youths had acted in his Court;
And straightway did his royal mandate send,
Commanding all his princes to attend; 40
All his wise men and captains he did call
Straight to assemble in the Council Hall:
The King himself in judgement takes his place,
And with his presence will the Senate grace;
His resolution doth to them declare
Impartially to end this nice affair.

And now the several writings being read,
That with the greater force they may proceed,
The King commands the young men in with speed,
And bids them freely speak their whole intent, 50
What either of them by his sentence meant:
And having leave, the first did silence break,
And to this purpose he before them spake.

Most mighty powers! doth not wine exceed
In strength? It overcometh all, indeed:

By freely drinking many are misled;
By wine the strongest have been conquered:
The needy orphan it will quickly bring
To be as gay and pleasant as the King;
Enslaveth him that heretofore was free; 60
Makes servants think they have their liberty;
The poor man and the rich alike are found,
While mirth and jollity go freely round;
Remembrance of all evils, past and gone,
Sorrows and debts, no more are thought upon,
When sparkling wine their heart begins to cheer,
Nor King, nor governor they seem to fear;
They speak at large, each would be chief of all,
Till friends and brethren at variance fall:
Drawn swords sometimes the pow'r of wine attend, 70
But when 'tis gone, the quarrel's at an end;
Their wrath forgot, their mirth thought on no more,
Each man is in the state he was before.
The force and pow'r of wine, consider'd well,
Must needs in strength all other things excel.

He having spoke, the second did begin
Thus to declare the power of the King.

THE THREE WISE SENTENCES

Most noble lords! Of all things that were made,
Or ever on the earth a being had,
Men do excel in strength: to their command   80
All things are subject, both by sea and land:
How strong, then, is the King, whose regal sway
All men on earth submissively obey!
They yield obedience to his princely will,
And ready are his pleasure to fulfil;
To his dominion high and low submit;
He over them bears rule as he thinks fit.
If he in hostile manner draws his sword,
Whole armed legions straight attend his word;
Whate'er he bids, they do with heart and hand −   90
Walls, tow'rs, nor bulwarks can before them stand;
When into foreign lands he doth them send,
They, in his quarrel, even their blood do spend,
And fight till vict'ry doth on them attend;
Then, with glad hearts, submissively they bring
The choicest spoils with homage to the King:
While those whose bus'ness is to till the ground,
With whom a sword or spear is seldom found,
Manure their land, their fruitful vineyards dress;

They reap their corn, and luscious clusters press: 100
And when the harvest doth their toil reward,
They bring their tribute to their sovereign lord.
If any hapless wretch the King displease,
His neighbours ne'er dispute, but on him seize;
If he bid spare, they spare; if he bid kill,
They ready are his pleasure to fulfil;
If cities to destroy, or buildings burn,
They into heaps of ruin kingdoms turn:
If clemency within his breast take place,
His people all adore his princely grace, 110
And build, and plant what late they did deface.
Whene'er he please he lays him down to sleep,
While armed bands strict watch do round him keep;
Nor dare depart, nor their own bus'ness mind,
But serve the King, as duty doth them bind.
Then what can equal him for strength, I pray –
Whom in such sort all men on earth obey?

Wise Zorabable then appears in place,
A royal youth of David's kingly race
(Much nobler he than those that spoke before, 120

THE THREE WISE SENTENCES

Because he did the living God adore),
And thus his mind and writing did declare
Before them all, that fate in judgement there.

Most worthy princes! I do freely own
The strength of kings throughout the world is known;
The force of wine all mortals know full well;
Yet neither of them doth in might excel:
Women alone must bear the prize away,
Whom all mankind do honour and obey.
And well they may, because from them do spring   130
The poor and rich, the peasant and the King;
The greatest heroes that the world can know
To women their original must owe;
They nourish those that plant the fruitful vine,
From whence you vainly boast the pow'r of wine;
The glory and the praise of men they are,
And make the garment which they daily wear;
Nay, without women, men can't be at all,
But soon the species would to ruin fall.
When men have gather'd gold, and treasures great,   140
Of precious things, and live in pomp and state,

THE WOMAN'S LABOUR

No true content their captive hearts attain
Unless they can a woman's favour gain;
Her beauty to adore they are inclin'd,
Her noble virtue does attract the mind;
With gold and silver they will freely part
To gain admission to a female's heart;
Her rare perfections are so much admir'd,
Nought in the world can be like her desir'd;
For if his native country lay at stake,   150
The husband quits it for his spouse's sake;
His parents, friends and kindred he doth leave;
Unto his wife alone his heart doth cleave:
Nought comes amiss, he's happy if he find
A consort virtuous, loving, fair and kind;
A willing homage he to her doth pay;
In toil and labour hard he spends the day,
To gather wealth, that so he may provide
Treasure to bring unto his dearest bride;
Another boldly, with a sword in hand,   160
Will cross the seas, and wander on the land;
No horrid dangers can procure his stay;
He bravely dares a lion in the way;

THE THREE WISE SENTENCES

Laden with booty to his mistress flies,
And at her feet presents the golden prize.
Some men, for love of women, oft we see
Have been reduc'd to utmost misery,
And lost their senses, if they chanc'd to find
A beauteous female cruel and unkind.
How oft have wretched mortals been misled,   170
With murd'rous hands their rival's blood to shed?
While some as desp'rately have sought for death,
And by self-murder stopt their vital breath!
The King is strong, no people can deny
The honours due to sovereign majesty:
All stand in fear of him; his pow'r is such
'Tis death to strike, no less than death to touch.
This mighty monarch I did lately spy
In's chair of state, fair Apame* sitting by;
At his right hand this youthful beauty bright   180
Appear'd like Cynthia's* glitt'ring rays of light;
Altho' he did the Persian sceptre sway,
This blooming lady took his crown away;
The diadem that on his head was worn,
Her lovely brows and temples did adorn;

Nay, furthermore, when she had done this thing,
With her left hand she struck this puissant King;
Yet no displeasure did in him arise,
Who was captive to her conqu'ring eyes:
Her radiant beauty did such beams display,   190
From her he could not turn his eyes away:
If this illustrious lady deign'd to smile,
Oe'rcome with joy, the King would laugh the while;
If ought displeas'd her, then the King would try
With gentle words the dame to pacify.
What mortal strength with women can compare,
Since crowned heads to them obedient are?

The King and princes then began to gaze,
And look upon each other with amaze;
For now they very plainly did descry   200
This noble prince would have the victory:
Who, having paus'd, began to speak again,
Not doubting but he should acceptance gain.

Most noble counsellors assembled here!
Women are strong, as I have made appear;

THE THREE WISE SENTENCES

The earth is large, wherein all creatures dwell;
The heavens stupendous doth in height excel;
The glorious sun does heat and light display,
And with his beams gives ev'ry region day:
How great, then, He, by whose divine command
All things at first were made – earth, sea and land!
Strong is the Truth, who did create all things;
From that blest fountain all perfection springs:
The heav'nly Host with rev'rence all adore,
While men on earth with trembling fear implore
Almighty Truth, which ever shall endure,
When worldly pomp and splendour are no more.

That kings are wicked, all wise men agree;
Women are so, we know assuredly;
When to excessive drinking men incline,
The worst of evils has been caus'd by wine:
All men on earth of high and low degree,
Are subject unto sin and vanity;
Destruction does on wickedness attend,
But mighty Truth shall never know an end;
Not only strong, but good beyond compare;

No wicked men with Him accepted are:
No rich reward, no golden bribe can buy
License from Truth to act unfaithfully:
Fraud or deceit in Truth we never find;   230
Good men embrace it with a ready mind:
Whatever thing is virtuous, good and great
In Truth we find it perfect and complete:
Then prais'd be Truth to all eternity,
In whom alone is strength and majesty!

He having finish'd, the attentive crowd
With joyful acclamations shout aloud;
The Truth applauding, they, as one, agree
This brave young prince should have the victory:
The King and council did his wisdom praise,   240
Affirming he had doubly won the bays.
Straightway the King Darius did declare
That purple* and fine linen he should wear,
That all his royal bounty might behold;
Commanded he should eat and drink in gold;
A regal chariot, too, he did decree,
Adorn'd with gold, at his command should be;

THE THREE WISE SENTENCES

A massy chain of gold his neck does grace,
And next unto himself assigns his place:
And to increase his honour, after all,   250
Commands that they his cousin should him call;
And of his royal grace he doth decree,
What he would ask, performed it should be:
'Speak what thou wilt, it shall be done for thee.'
He was not long to seek what choice to make,
But to the King with low submission spake.

Most mighty Prince! I beg thou wouldst pursue
The thing that thou proposedst long ago.
Behold Jerusalem in ruins laid!
Perform the vow which thou thyself hast made,   260
When first thou didst the Persian sceptre wield –
That thou the peerless city wouldst rebuild;
That glorious temple, which was once the praise
Of all the earth, thou vowdst again to raise;
That goodly pile by Edomites* destroy'd,
Each goodly building now in ashes laid,
And all the holy vessels to restore,
As Cyrus* did design long time before;

That then Judea's sons may bless thy name,
And babes unborn thy matchless grace proclaim.   270
No other thing, great Prince, do I require;
No earthly pomp or grandeur I desire:
But if this one request thou grant to me,
Immortal honour thy reward will be.

The King, observing how he stood inclin'd
To serve his country with a willing mind,
Rose from his seat, and in that very place,
Before the council, doth the prince embrace;
Grants his request, and doth his letters send,
Commanding all his captains to attend   280
Both him and his, that so they might convey
Them to their ancient land without delay:
Not only from all tribute set them free,
But gave much treasure to them lib'rally;
The city built, the temple up did raise,
For solemn worship, as in former days.
This brave young man, having his end obtain'd,
And liberty, beyond his wishes gain'd;
With thankful heart, and joyful lips, did raise
His voice to sing his great Creator's praise.   290

THE THREE WISE SENTENCES

To thee, great God! I render praises due,
From whom comes victory, and wisdom, too:
Thy worthless servant I myself do own,
Yet thou to me thy strength and might hast shown
Thine be the glory, now and evermore!
I thankfully thy gracious name adore;
Prostrate before thee would I gladly lie,
And praise thy name to all eternity.

THE THRESHER'S LABOUR

To the Revd. Mr Stanley*

The grateful tribute of these rural lays,
    Which to her patron's hand the muse conveys,
    Deign to accept: 'tis just she tribute bring
To him, whose bounty gives her life to sing;
To him, whose gen'rous favours tune her voice;
And bid her, 'midst her poverty, rejoice.
Inspir'd by these, she dares herself prepare
To sing the toils of each revolving year;
Those endless toils, which always grow anew,
And the poor thresher's destin'd to pursue: 10
Ev'n these, with pleasure, can the muse rehearse,
When you and gratitude demand her verse.

Soon as the golden harvest quits the plain,
And Ceres'* gifts reward the farmer's pain;
What corn each sheaf will yield, intent to hear,

And guess from thence the profits of the year,
He calls his reapers forth: around we stand,
With deep attention, waiting his command.
To each our task he readily divides,
And pointing, to our diff'rent stations guides. 20
As he directs, to distant barns we go;
Here two for wheat, and there for barley two.
But first, to show what he expects to find,
These words, or words like these, disclose his mind:

'So dry the corn was carry'd from the field,
So easily 'twill thresh, so well 'twill yield;
Sure large days' works I well may hope for now:
Come, strip and try – let's see what you can do.'

Divested of our clothes, with flail in hand,
At proper distance, front to front we stand: 30
And first the threshal's* gently swung, to prove
Whether with just exactness it will move:
That once secure, we swiftly whirl them round;
From the strong planks our crab-tree staves rebound,
And echoing barns return the rattling sound.

THE THRESHER'S LABOUR

Now in the air our knotty weapons fly,
And now with equal force descend from high;
Down one, one up, so well they keep the time,
The Cyclops' hammers* could not truer chime;
Nor with more heavy strokes could Etna groan,   40
When Vulcan forg'd the arms for Thetis' son.*
In briny streams our sweat descends apace,
Drops from our locks, or trickles down our face.
No intermission in our work we know;
The noisy threshal must forever go.
Their master absent, others safely play;
The sleeping threshal does itself betray.
Nor yet, the tedious labour to beguile,
And make the passing minutes sweetly smile,
Can we, like shepherds, tell a merry tale;   50
The voice is lost, drown'd by the louder flail.
But we may think: alas! what pleasing thing
Here to the mind can the dull fancy bring?
Our eye beholds no pleasing object here,
No cheerful sound diverts our list'ning ear.
The shepherd well may tune his voice to sing,
Inspir'd with all the beauties of the spring.
No fountains murmur here, no lambkins play,

No linnets warble, and no fields look gay;
'Tis all a gloomy, melancholy scene,
Fit only to provoke the muse's spleen.
When sooty peas we thresh, you scarce can know
Our native colour, as from work we go.
The sweat, the dust and suffocating smoke
Make us so much like Ethiopians look,
We scare our wives when ev'ning brings us home,
And frighted infants think the bugbear come.
Week after week, we this dull task pursue,
Unless when winn'wing* days produce a new –
A new, indeed, but frequently a worse!
The threshal yields but to the master's curse.
He counts the bushels, counts how much a day;
Then swears we've idled half our time away:
'Why, look ye, rogues, d'ye think that this will do?
Your neighbours thresh as much again as you.'
Now in our hands we wish our noisy tools
To drown the hated names of rogues and fools.
But wanting these, we just like schoolboys look,
When angry masters view the blotted book:
They cry, 'Their ink was faulty, and their pen!'
We: 'the corn threshes bad – 'twas cut too green.'

THE THRESHER'S LABOUR

But soon as winter hides his hoary head,
And nature's face is with new beauty spread,
The lovely spring appears: refreshing show'rs
New-clothe the field with grass and blooming flow'rs.
Next her, the rip'ning summer presses on,
And Sol begins his longest race to run.
Before the door our welcome master stands,
Tells us the ripen'd grass requires our hands.
The grateful tidings presently imparts 90
Life to our looks, and spirits to our hearts.
We wish the happy season may be fair;
And, joyful, long to breathe in op'ner air.
This change of labour seems to give such ease,
With thoughts of happiness ourselves we please.
But, ah! how rarely's happiness complete!
There's always bitter mingled with the sweet.
When first the lark sings prologue to the day,
We rise, admonish'd by his early lay;
This new employ with eager haste to prove, 100
This new employ, become so much our love.
Alas! that human joys should change so soon!
Our morning pleasure turns to pain at noon.

The birds salute us, as to work we go,
And with new life our bosoms seem to glow.
On our right shoulder hangs the crooked blade,
The weapon destin'd to unclothe the mead:
Our left supports the whetstone, scrip and beer;
This for our scythes, and these ourselves to cheer.
And now the field, design'd to try our might,   110
At length appears, and meets our longing sight.
The grass and ground we view with careful eyes,
To see which way the best advantage lies;
And, hero-like, each claims the foremost place.
At first our labour seems a sportive race:
With rapid force our sharpen'd blades we drive;
Strain ev'ry nerve, and blow for blow we give.
All strive to vanquish, tho' the victor gains
No other glory, but the greatest pains.

But when the scorching sun is mounted high,   120
And no kind barns with friendly shade are nigh,
Our weary scythes entangle in the grass,
While streams of sweat run trickling down apace.
Our sportive labour we too late lament;
And wish that strength again we vainly spent.

Thus, in the morn, a courser have I seen
With headlong fury scour the level green;
Or mount the hills, if hills are in his way,
As if no labour could his fire allay;
Till Phoebus, shining with meridian heat, 130
Has bath'd his panting sides in briny sweat:
The lengthen'd chase scarce able to sustain,
He measures back the hills and dales with pain.

With heat and labour tir'd, our scythes we quit,
Search out a shady tree, and down we sit:
From scrip and bottle hope new strength to gain;
But scrip and bottle too are try'd in vain.
Down our parch'd throats we scarce the bread can get;
And, quite o'erspent with toil, but faintly eat.
Nor can the bottle only answer all; 140
The bottle and the beer are both too small.
Time flows: again we rise from off the grass;
Again each mower takes his proper place;
Not eager now, as late, our strength to prove;
But all contented regular to move.
We often whet, and often view the sun;

As often wish his tedious race was run.
At length he veils his purple face from sight,
And bids the weary labourer goodnight.
Homewards we move, but spent so much with toil, 150
We slowly walk, and rest at ev'ry stile.
Our good expecting wives, who think we stay,
Got to the door, soon eye us in the way.
Then from the pot the dumplin's catch'd in haste,
And homely by its side the bacon plac'd.
Supper and sleep by morn new strength supply;
And out we set again, our work to try;
But not so early quite, nor quite so fast,
As, to our cost, we did the morning past.

Soon as the rising sun has drank the dew, 160
Another scene is open to our view:
Our master comes, and at his heels a throng
Of prattling females, arm'd with rake and prong,
Prepar'd, whilst he is here, to make his hay,
Or, if he turns his back, prepar'd to play;
But here, or gone, sure of this comfort still,
Here's company, so they may chat their fill.

Ah! were their hands so active as their tongues,
How nimbly then would move the rakes and prongs?

The grass again is spread upon the ground,   170
Till not a vacant place is to be found;
And while the parching sunbeams on it shine,
The haymakers have time allow'd to dine.
That soon dispatch'd, they still sit on the ground;
And the brisk chat, renew'd, afresh goes round.
All talk at once; but seeming all to fear,
That what they speak, the rest will hardly hear;
Till by degrees so high their notes they strain,
A stander-by can nought distinguish plain.
So loud's their speech, and so confus'd their noise,   180
Scarce puzzled Echo* can return the voice.
Yet, spite of this, they bravely all go on;
Each scorns to be, or seem to be, outdone.
Meanwhile, the changing sky begins to lour,
And hollow winds proclaim a sudden show'r:
The tattling crowd can scarce their garments gain
Before descends the thick impetuous rain;
Their noisy prattle all at once is done,
And to the hedge they soon for shelter run.

Thus have I seen, on a bright summer's day,
On some green brake a flock of sparrows play;
From twig to twig, from bush to bush they fly;
And with continu'd chirping fill the sky:
But, on a sudden, if a storm appears,
Their chirping noise no longer dins your ears:
They fly for shelter to the thickest bush;
There silent sit, and all at once is hush.

But better fate succeeds this rainy day,
And little labour serves to make the hay.
Fast as 'tis cut, so kindly shines the sun,
Turn'd once or twice, the pleasing work is done.
Next day the cocks appear in equal rows,
Which the glad master in safe ricks bestows.

The spacious fields we now no longer range;
And yet, hard fate! still work for work we change.
Back to the barns we hastily are sent,
Where lately so much time we pensive spent:
Not pensive now, we bless the friendly shade;
And to avoid the parching sun are glad.

Yet little time we in the shade remain 210
Before our master calls us forth again,
And says: 'For harvest now yourselves prepare;
The ripen'd harvest now demands your care.
Get all things ready, and be quickly dresst;
Early next morn I shall disturb your rest.'
Strict to his word! for scarce the dawn appears
Before his hasty summons fills our ears.
His hasty summons we obey; and rise,
While yet the stars are glimm'ring in the skies.
With him our guide we to the wheat field go, 220
He to appoint, and we the work to do.

Ye reapers, cast your eyes around the field,
And view the various scenes its beauties yield:
Then look again, with a more tender eye,
To think how soon it must in ruin lie!
For, once set in, where'er our blows we deal,
There's no resisting of the well-whet steel:
But here or there, where'er our course we bend,
Sure desolation does our steps attend.

THE WOMAN'S LABOUR

Thus, when Arabia's sons, in hopes of prey, 230
To some more fertile country take their way,
How beauteous all things in the morn appear!
There rural cots, and pleasant villas here!
So many grateful objects meet the sight,
The ravish'd eye could willing gaze till night.
But long ere then, where'er their troops have past,
These pleasing prospects lie a gloomy waste.

The morning past, we sweat beneath the sun;
And but uneasily our work goes on.
Before us we perplexing thistles find, 240
And corn blown adverse with the ruffling wind.
Behind our master waits; and if he spies
One charitable ear, he grudging cries,
'Ye scatter half your wages o'er the land,'
Then scrapes the stubble with his greedy hand.

Let those who feast at ease on dainty fare
Pity the reapers who their feasts prepare:
For toils scarce ever ceasing press us now;
Rest never does, but on the Sabbath, show;

THE THRESHER'S LABOUR

And barely that our masters will allow. 250
Think what a painful life we daily lead:
Each morning early rise, go late to bed;
Nor, when asleep, are we secure from pain:
We then perform our labours o'er again;
Our mimic fancy ever restless seems;
And what we act awake, she acts in dreams.
Hard fate! our labours ev'n in sleep don't cease;
Scarce Hercules e'er felt such toils as these!

But soon we rise the bearded crop again;
Soon Phoebus' rays well dry the golden grain. 260
Pleas'd with the scene, our master glows with joy;
Bids us for carrying all our force employ;
When strait confusion o'er the field appears,
And stunning clamours fill the workmen's ears;
The bells and clashing whips alternate sound,
And rattling wagons thunder o'er the ground.
The wheat, when carry'd, peas and other grain,
We soon secure, and leave a fruitless plain;
In noisy triumph the last load moves on,
And loud huzzas proclaim the harvest done. 270

Our master, joyful at the pleasing sight,
Invites us all to feast with him at night.
A table plentifully spread we find,
And jugs of humming ale, to cheer the mind;
Which he, too gen'rous, pushes round so fast,
We think no toils to come, nor mind the past.
But the next morning soon reveals the cheat,
When the same toils we must again repeat;
To the same barns must back again return,
To labour there for room for next year's corn. 280

Thus, as the year's revolving course goes round,
No respite from our labour can be found:
Like Sisyphus, our work is never done;
Continually rolls back the restless stone.
New-growing labours still succeed the past;
And growing always new, must always last.

AN ELEGY
UPON STEPHEN DUCK

In murmuring strains, I lately heard it said,
   The muse's darling, Reverend Duck, is dead.
   Impartial death by one untimely blow
Has snatch'd away from mortals here below
That wond'rous man, in whom alone did join
A thresher, poet, courtier and divine.
And while a labourer of mean degree,
The ornament, and grace of poverty
Upon that state in high and lofty rhyme,
Bravely attempts Parnassus' Hill* to climb;   10
And quickly after by fame's loud report
Remov'd from his lowly cot and call'd to Court.
A gracious queen being charm'd with the lyre,

While noble peers his nat'ral parts admire;
Advanc'd, caress'd and favour'd more and more,
Nor ceased till the rev'rend gown he wore.
Immortal Duck, how happy hadst thou been –
Belov'd by lords, respected by a queen?
How doubly blest couldst thou have kept with thee,
The sweet companion of thy poverty? 20
That true content and inward peace of mind,
Which in thy humble cottage thou didst find.
Which oft doth to the poor and mean retreat
But seldom dwells among the rich or great.
The want of wit thy pleasure turn'd to pain,
Thy life a burden, and thy death a stain:
So have I seen in a fair summer's morn,
Bright Phoebus' beams the hills and dales adorn,
With flow'rs and shrubs their fragrant sweets display,
And warbling birds foretell a cheerful day: 30
When on a sudden some dark clouds arise,
Obscures the sun and overspreads the skies;
The birds are silent, plants contract their bloom,
The glorious day ends in a dismal gloom.

AN EPISTOLARY ANSWER

To an exciseman who doubted
her being the author of
The Woman's Labour

Good sir, by our English laws
The accused party may
Have leave to plead, themselves to clear,
But you condemn straightway.

Unseen, unheard, the sentence past,
For you are sure, I hear,
No woman ever made those lines
That in my name appear.

But I'm much more sure that you
For once mistaken are;
You are not infallible, nor fit
To fill the papal chair.

For there is none on earth below,
Nor yet above the sky,
Can truly say they made that book
But poor, despised I.

And whether you believe or not,
The thing is certain true:
That washerwoman made those lines
That now are sent to you.

Tho' my extraction was so low,
And I to labour bred,
Yet stories of the pagan gods
I oft have seen and read.

And were you now in Petersfield,
Or I in Gloucestershire,

AN EPISTOLARY ANSWER

What you have judg'd impossible
I wou'd plainly make appear.

But why shou'd you our sex condemn,
And women all despise? 30
We never with you interfere,
Nor trouble the excise.

I wonder much, indeed to find
That such your notions are,
For most of you are wont to be
Admirers of the fair.

But since that we such idiots are,
I hope, you do refrain
Our company, for fear you shou'd
Your reputation stain. 40

Tho' if we education had
Which justly is our due,
I doubt not many of our sex
Might fairly vie with you.

NOTE ON THE TEXTS

The text of *The Woman's Labour* in this edition is based on that of the first edition of the pamphlet, which was published in 1739. *The Thresher's Labour* was first published in 1730, although the text in this edition is based on the later edition published in *Poems on Several Occasions* in 1736, which is considered the authoritative text. Capitalisation, italicisation, spelling, punctuation and grammar have been silently corrected throughout to make the text more appealing to the modern reader. The italics in Collier's texts are original.

NOTES

9 *the Nine*: The nine muses in Greek and Roman mythology.
9 *advanc'd by Caroline*: A reference to Queen Caroline, who was Duck's patron until her death in 1737 – she gave Duck an annuity and a house, and in 1733 made him a Yeoman of the Guard.
10 *Jove*: Jove is another name for Jupiter, the Roman god of the sky and thunder.
10 *Danaë*: In Greek mythology, Danaë is a princess, and is the mother of Perseus.

10 *Alcides*: Another name for Hercules; in *The Thresher's Labour*, Duck says 'Scarce Hercules e'er felt such toils as these!' (see line 258 on p. 53).

10 *your annual task*: i.e. the harvest, the subject of *The Thresher's Labour*.

14 *Titan's golden rays*: In Greek mythology, the Titans were the pre-Olympian gods. 'Titan' is used poetically to personify the sun (Hyperion, one of the Titans, was the father of Helios, the sun god).

15 *Orion*: A reference to the constellation; i.e. night-time.

16 *Cambrics*: A fine white linen, often used for making handkerchiefs.

17 *Sol*: The sun in Roman mythology.

20 *Sisyphus*: In Greek mythology, Sisyphus is condemned in Hades to the eternal task of pushing a boulder up a hill, only for it to roll back down again.

20 *Danaus' daughters*: In Greek mythology, Danaus, King of Libya, had fifty daughters, who were known as the Danaides; the daughters were punished in Tartarus, where they were forced to carry water in a jug and fill a bath; the bath had a leak, and so, much like Sisyphus, their task was never complete.

21 *Book of Esdras*: Esdras is a Greek variation of the name Ezra; 1 Esdras is an ancient Greek version of the Book of Ezra from the Bible.

23 *great Darius, Persia's royal king*: Darius the Great was the third Persian King of Kings (r. 522 BC–486 BC).

24 *Aurora*: The Roman goddess of the dawn.

24 *Phoebus*: A reference to Apollo, the god of the sun.

31 *Apame*: The King's concubine in 1 Esdras.

NOTES

31 *Cynthia*: A reference to the moon; the Greek Selene and the Roman Diana, goddesses of the moon, were sometimes referred to as Cynthia.

34 *purple*: The colour purple ('Tyrian purple') was usually reserved for those of high rank.

35 *Behold Jerusalem... Edomites*: A reference to the siege of Jerusalem by Nebuchadnezzar II, which began in 589 BC.

35 *Cyrus*: Cyrus the Great, or Cyrus II of Persia, was the founder of the first Persian empire.

39 *Revd. Mr Stanley*: Another of Duck's patrons (see also second note to p. 9), Revered Stanley suggested to Duck that he wrote about his own life.

41 *Ceres*: The Roman goddess of agriculture.

42 *threshal*: A threshal, or flail, is a wooden stave with a short stick swinging from it.

43 *Cyclops' hammers*: In the poetry of Callimachus (*c*.305–*c*.240 BC), three Cyclops, Brontes, Steropes and Arges, become assistants at to the Greek god of blacksmiths, Hephaestus.

43 *Etna groan... Thetis' son*: A reference to Vulcan, the Roman equivalent of Hephaestus, who made a suit of armour for Achilles, the son of Thetis. Vulcan's forge was located under Mount Etna.

44 *winn'wing*: To winnow is to expose grain to the wind so that the lighter chaff is blown away.

49 *Echo*: In Greek mythology, Echo was a mountain nymph who was condemned by Hera to only speak the last words she heard.

55 *Parnassus' Hill*: A reference to Mount Parnassus, a mountain in central Greece which was sacred in Greek mythology.

OTHER CLASSIC POETRY FROM RENARD PRESS

ISBN: 9781913724153
10pp hardback concertina • £2.50

Bars Fight, *a ballad telling the tale of an ambush by Native Americans on two families in 1746 in a Massachusetts meadow, is the oldest known work by an African-American author. Passed on orally until it was recorded in Josiah Gilbert Holland's* History of Western Massachusetts *in 1855, the ballad is a landmark in the history of literature that should be on every book lover's shelves.*

In 1773, Poems on Various Subjects, Religious and Moral *became the first book of poetry by an African-American author to be published. At the tender age of seven, Phillis had been brought to Massachusetts as a slave and sold to the well-to-do Wheatley family. There, she threw herself into education, and soon she was devouring the classics and writing verse with whatever she had to hand – odes in chalk on the walls of the house. This edition also includes an 1834 memoir by an outspoken proponent of antislavery, B.B. Thatcher.*

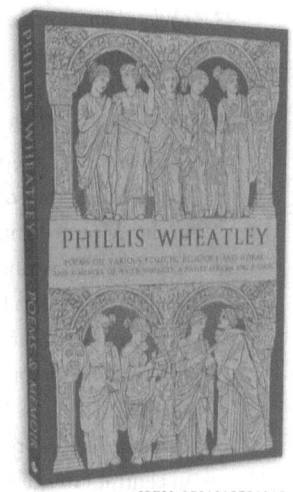

ISBN: 9781913724146
128pp paperback • £8.99

DISCOVER THE FULL COLLECTION AT
WWW.RENARDPRESS.COM

www.ingramcontent.com/pod-product-compliance
Lightning Source LLC
Chambersburg PA
CBHW011318080526
44589CB00020B/2751